Are You Broke?
Think Again

By

Roshdy Ebrahim, Ph.D

2020

Are you broke? Think again

Roshdy Ebrahim

Contents

Chapter 1
An honest look at the personal finance crisis [1]

You know me. I am in your friendship circle hidden in plain sight. My clothes are still impeccable -- bought in the good years when I was still making money. To look at me you would not know that my electricity was cut off last week for nonpayment, or that I meet the eligibility requirements for food stamps. But if you paid attention, you would see that sadness in my eyes -- hear that hint of fear in my otherwise self-assured voice.

These days I'm buying the $1.99 trial-size jug of Tide to make ends meet. I bet you didn't know laundry detergent came in that size. You invite me to the same expensive restaurants the two of us have always enjoyed, but I order mineral water now with a twist of lemon, not the 12-dollar glass of chardonnay. I am frugal in my menu choices. Meticulous, I count every penny in my

---

[1] Elizabeth white: 55, Underemployed, and Faking Normal: Your Guide to a Better Life. Amazon, 2019

head. I demur dividing the table bill evenly to cover desserts and designer coffees and second and third glasses of wine I did not consume.

I am tired of trying to fake appearances. A friend told me that I'm broke not poor, and there is a difference. I live without cable, my gym membership and nail appointments. I've discovered I can do my own hair. There is no retirement savings, no nest egg. I exhausted that long ago. There is no expensive condo to draw equity and no husband to back me up. Months of slow pay and no pay have decimated my credit. Bill collectors call constantly, reading verbatim from a script before expressing polite sympathy for my plight and then demanding payment arrangements I can't possibly meet. Friends wonder privately how someone so well educated could be in economic free fall.

I'm still as talented as ever and smart as a whip, but work is sketchy now, mostly on and off consulting gigs. At 55 I've learned how to fake cheeriness, but there are not many opportunities for work anymore. I don't remember exactly when it stopped, but I cannot deny now having entered the uncertain world of formerly and used to be. I'm not sure anymore where I belong. What I do know is that dozens of online job applications seem to just disappear into a black hole. I'm wondering what is to become of me. So far my health has held up, but my body aches -- or is it my spirit? Homeless women used to be invisible to me but I appraise them now with curious eyes, wondering if their stories started like mine.

I wrote this piece a year ago. It's a composite of my story and other women I know. I wrote it because I was tired of pretending, I was all right when I wasn't. I was tired of faking normal. I wasn't seeing myself in the popular press. Nobody I knew was traveling the world or buying a condo in Costa Rica. Very few of my friends had set aside the 15 to 20 percent experts tell us we need to maintain our standard of living in retirement. My friends, many in their 50s and 60s, were looking at a downward mobility, a work-for-life proposition, just a job loss, medical diagnosis or divorce away from insolvency. We may not have hit rock bottom, but many of us saw a sequence of events where rock bottom was possible for the first time.

And the truth is, it really doesn't take much. The median household in the US only has enough savings to replace one month of income. Forty-seven percent of us cannot pull together 400 dollars to deal with an emergency. That's almost half of us. A major car repair and we're standing on the abyss. You wouldn't know it to look around you -- I'm not the only one in this situation. There are people in this room who are in the same predicament, and if it's not you, it is your parents or your sister or maybe your best friend. We get good at faking normal. Shame keeps us silent and siloed. When I first decided I was going to come out with my story, I did a website and a friend noticed that there were no photos of me -- it was all kind of cartoons like this. Even as I was coming out, I was still hiding.

We live in a world where success is defined by income. When you say that you have money problems, you're announcing pretty much that you're a loser. When you're a graduate of Harvard Business School as I am, you're some kind of double loser.

We boomers hear a lot about how we have underfunded our retirement; how it's all our fault. Why on earth would we draw down our 401(k) plan to cover the shortfall on our mother-in-law's nursing home care, or to pay for our kid's tuition, or just to survive? We're accused of being poor planners and deadbeats -- all that money we spent on lattes and bottled water. To shame and blame is so deliciously tempting. Many of us don't even wait for others to do it we're so busy doing it to ourselves. I say let's own our part: we all could have saved more. I know I could have saved more, and if you were to rifle through my life over the last 30 years, you would see more than one dumb thing I have done financially. I can't change that now and neither can you, but let's not mix up individual, isolated behavior with the systemic factors that have caused a 7.7-trillion-dollar retirement income gap.

Millions of boomer-age Americans did not land here because of too many trips to Starbucks. We spent the last three decades dealing with flat and falling wages and disappearing pensions and through-the-roof cost on housing and health care and education. It used to not be like this. We all remember the three-legged retirement income stool which had the savings and pension and social security. Well, that stool has gone wobbly.

Take savings -- what savings? For many families, there's just nothing left to save after the bills have been paid. The pension leg of the stool has also gone wobbly. We can remember when many people had pensions. Today only 13 percent of American workers are employed by companies that offer them. So, what did we get instead? We got 401(k)-type plans and suddenly responsibility for retirement planning got shifted from our companies to us. We got the reigns but we also got the risk, and it turns out that millions of us just aren't that good at voluntarily investing over 40 years. Millions of us just aren't that good at managing market risk. And really the numbers tell the story. Half of all-American households have no retirement savings at all. That would be zero. No 401(k), no IRA, not a dime. Among 55-to-64-year-olds who do have a retirement account, the median value of that account is 104,000 dollars. Now, 104,000 dollars does sound better than zero, but as an annuity, it generates about 300 dollars. I don't have to tell you that you can't live on that.

With savings down, pensions becoming a relic of the past and 401(k) plans failing millions of Americans, many near-retirees are dependent on social security as their retirement plan. But here's the problem. Social security was never supposed to be the retirement plan. It's not nearly enough. At best it replaces something like 40 percent of your pre-retirement income.

Things have changed a lot from when social security was introduced back in 1935. Then, a 21-year-old male had a 50 percent chance of living until he was 65. So, he retired at 60, did a little fishing, kissed his grandkids, got his gold watch -- he'd be dead within five years of receiving benefits. That's not the pattern today. If you're in your late 50s and in good health, you're going to live easily another 20 or 25 years. That's a really long time to make ends meet if you are broke.

So, what's the play if you've landed here and you're 50 or 55 or 60? What's the play if you don't want to land here and you're 22 or 32? Here's what I've learned from my own experience. The cavalry's not coming. There is no big rescue, no prince charming, no big bailout in the works. To have a shot at something other than being old and poor in America, we're going to have to save ourselves and each other. I've had to come out of the shadows, stand here openly, and I'm inviting you to do so as well. I'm not going to tell you that it's not easy. I ventured though to tell my story because I thought it would make it a little easier for people to tell theirs. I think it's only through our strength in numbers that we can begin to change the national "la-la" conversation that we are having on this retirement crisis. With so many of us shell-shocked and adrift about what has happened to us, we're going to have to build up from the grassroots, forming what I think are resilience circles. These are small groups of people coming together to talk about what has happened to them, to share resources and information and to begin to figure out a way forward. I believe from this base that we can find our voices again and sound the alarm -- start pushing our institutions and policymakers to go hard on this retirement crisis with the urgency it deserves.

In the meantime -- and there is an "in the meantime" -- we're going to have to adopt a live-low-to-the-ground mindset, drastically cutting back on our expenses. And I don't mean just living within our means. A lot of people are already doing that. What is called for now is to, in a much deeper way, ask ourselves what it really means to live a life that is not defined by things. I call it "smalling up." Smalling up is figuring out what you really need to feel contented and grounded. I have a friend who drives really beat-up, raggedy cars, but he will scrimp and save 15,000 dollars at one point to buy a flute because music is what really matters to him. He smalled up.

I've had to also let go of magical thinking -- this idea that if I just was patient enough and tightened my belt that things would go back to normal. If I just sent in one more CV or applied to one more job online or attended one more networking event that surely, I'd get the kind of job I was used to having. Surely things would return to normal. The truth is I'm not going back and neither are you. The normal that we knew is over. In this new place that we are, we're going to be asked to do things that we don't want to do. We're going to be asked to take assignments that we think are beneath our station and our talent and our skill. I have had to get off my throne. Last year, a good friend of mine asked me if I would help her with some organization work. I assumed she meant community organizing along the lines of what President Obama did in Chicago. She meant organizing somebody's closet. I said, "I'm not doing that." She said, "Get off your throne. Money is green."

It's not easy being part of the advance team that is ushering in this new era of work and living. First is always hardest. First is before there are networks and pathways and role models ... before there are policies and ways to show us how to go forward. We're in the middle of a seismic shift, and we're going to have to find bridgework to get us through. Bridgework is what we do in the meantime; bridgework is what we do while we're trying to figure out what is next. Bridgework is also letting go of this notion that our worth and our value depend on our income and our titles and our jobs. Bridgework can look crazy or cool depending on how you were rolling when your personal financial crisis hit. I have friends with PhDs who are working at the Container Store or driving Uber or Lyft, and then I have other friends who are partnering with other boomers and doing really cool entrepreneurial ventures. Bridgework doesn't mean that we don't want to build on our past careers, that we don't want meaningful work. We do. Bridgework is what we do in the meantime while we're figuring out what is next.

I've also learned to think strategy not failure when I'm sort of processing all these things that I don't want to do. And I say that that's an approach that I would invite you to consider as well.

So, if you need to move in with your brother to make ends meet, call him. If you need to take in a boarder to help you pay your mortgage or pay your rent, do it. If you need to get food stamps, get the darn food stamps. AARP says only a third of older adults who are eligible actually get them. Do what you need to do to go another round. Know that there are millions of us. Come out of the shadows. Cut back, small up; think strategy, not failure; get off your throne and find the bridgework to get your through the lean times.

As a country, we have achieved longevity, investing billions of dollars in the diagnosis, treatment and management of disease. It's not enough to just live a long time. We want to live well. We haven't invested nearly as much in the physical infrastructure to ensure that that happens. We need now a new way of thinking about what it means to be old in America. And we need guidance and ideas about how to live a richly textured life on a much more modest income.

So, I am calling on change agents and social entrepreneurs, artists and elders and impact investors. I'm calling on developers and disrupters of the status quo. We need you to help us imagine how to invest in the services and products and infrastructure that will support our dignity, our independence and our well-being in these many, many decades that we're going to live.

My journey has taken me from a place of fear and shame to one of humility and understanding. I'm ready now to link shields with others, to fight this fight, and I'm inviting you to join me.

Chapter 2
Let's get honest about our money problems [2]

Have you ever had to break your family's rules? Today, I'm breaking mine, around money, secrecy and shame. In 2006, on my brother Keith's 40th birthday, he called. "Tam, I'm in dire straits. I wouldn't ask unless I had to. Can I borrow 7,500 dollars?" This wasn't the first time he needed quick cash, but this time, his voice frightened me. I had never heard him so beaten down and shameful, and it was on his 40th birthday.

After a few basic questions that we would all ask, I agreed to loan him the money, but under one condition: that as the financial professional in the family, I wanted to meet with him and his wife to see what was really happening.

Weeks later, we met at the local Starbucks, and I started right in with the tough-

---

[2] tammy lally: money coach.

love budget conversation. "You should sell the house, downsize to something you can afford, sell the toys. And Starbucks? Give up the five-dollar-a-day coffee."

You know, all the trappings that we do to keep up with the Joneses. Quickly, my brother and his wife went into a fearsome blame game, and it got messy. I vacillated between therapist and pissed-off sister. I wanted them to be better than this.

"Come on, you two. Get your shit together. You're parents. Grow up and buck up." After we left, I called my mom, but Keith beat me to it, and he told her that I wasn't helpful. In fact, he was hurt and felt ganged-up on. Of course, he did. I shamed him with my tough-love budget conversation.

Two months went by when I received a call. "Tam? I have bad news. Keith committed suicide last night." Days later, at his home, I went looking for answers, in his "office" -- the garage. There, I found a stack of overdue credit card bills and a foreclosure notice served to him on the day that he died. My brother left behind his beautiful 10-year-old daughter, his brilliant 18-year-old son, weeks before his high school graduation, and his wife of 20 years.

How did this happen? My brother was caught in our family's money-shame cycle, and he was far from alone in this. Suicide rates among adults ages 40 to 64 have risen nearly 40 percent since 1999. Job loss, bankruptcy and foreclosures were present in nearly 40 percent of the deaths, with white middle-aged men accounting for seven out of 10 suicides.

What I've learned is that our self-destructive and self-defeating financial behaviors are not driven by our rational, logical minds. Instead, they are a product of our subconscious belief systems rooted in our childhoods and so deeply ingrained in us, they shape the way that we deal with money our entire adult lives, and so many of you are left believing that you're lazy, crazy or stupid -- or just bad with money.

This is what I call money shame. Dr. Brené Brown, a well-known shame researcher, defines shame as "the intensely painful feeling or experience of believing that we are flawed, and therefore unworthy of love and belonging." Based on this definition, here's how I'm defining money shame: "the intensely painful feeling or experience of believing that we are flawed, and therefore unworthy of love and belonging, based on our bank account balances, our debts, our homes, our cars and our job titles."

Let me give you a couple of examples of what I mean. I believe that we all have money shame, whether you earn 10,000 dollars a year or 10 million, and it's because we give money all of our power. Here's what it would look like if someone that you love, or you, might have money shame. They play the big shot, always picking up the check, financially rescuing family and friends.

They are financially secure, but they live in a state of chronic not-enoughness. They drive a Mercedes, but their budget really only can afford a Honda. And they're looking good at every cost.

I know that we can break free from the grips of money shame, because I did. Shortly after my brother's death, the Recession hit. I lost my business and faced bankruptcy. Secretly, I was terrified. I stayed in my home for a year, thinking I did something wrong, told myself, "What did you do? What happened?" I stayed silent, while all along, I went outside and smiled. Nobody knew. That's money shame.

So, what I had to do was let go of the grip that I had on knowing all the answers. I was the know-it-all in my family, and I had to give up the idea that a new financial plan was the solution. And so just like everything in my life, for me, I was sent a human to help, and I accepted the help, but I had to do major self-inquiry about my family's money history and my money beliefs.

We have to start having this conversation. Money can no longer be a taboo topic. We have to get honest with each other that we're suffering with money issues, and let's get real -- we have to stop numbing out our pain. In order to uncover the painful parts of your money story and your money history, you can't be numb. We have to let go of our past in order to be free. Letting go of the past happens through surrender, faith and forgiveness.

Debt is the tangible manifestation of not forgiving. If you have debt, you've not completely forgiven your past, so it's our work to forgive ourselves and others so that we can live freely. Otherwise, our history will continue to repeat. This is not a quick fix, and I know we all want one, but it's a slow wake-up. This is another level of work. We have to go higher to get it, to get at it.

So, try this: follow your dollars. Your money will show you right away what you value. Where's it going? And then ask yourself: Do I really value all this stuff? And get curious about what you're feeling when you're spending. Are you lonely? Are you bored? Or are you just excited?

But there's deeper work that needs to happen. How did you get all these money beliefs to begin with? I call this your money autobiography, and as a money coach, this is the first step I take with my clients.

Think back to your earliest childhood money memory. What did it feel like when you got money? Were you excited, proud or confused? And what did you do with the money? Did you run with the candy store, or did you run to the bank? And what did you hear your parents say, and what did you see your parents do with the money?

My brother and I heard, "More money will make us happy." Every day. "More money will make us happy." And we internalized that into the money belief that our self-worth was equal to our net worth as we watched our mom live in a state of chronic not-enoughness. And she numbed the pain with sugar and shopping.

So, what did we do? Keith played out my mother's life. He was an underearner, longed to be financially rescued, and he numbed out the pain with alcohol. I did the opposite. I became a high earner, rescuer, and I numbed the pain out with self-help books. But what we had in common was our money belief. We both believed that our bank account balance was equal to our self-worth.

Looking back at the Starbucks meeting with my brother ... he didn't need a budget and my judgment. He needed a breakthrough from his suffering, and he needed my compassion. Keith was not able to be the one to speak up and break our family money shame cycle, so he left me to do the work and share his legacy. Change is difficult, but in my family, not changing is fatal.

So, I did the work, and I have experienced deep and profound forgiveness, and as I stand here today, I am living on purpose, I serve, and money serves me. It only takes one person in your family to break through the money-shame cycle. I want you to be the one.

Chapter 3
A monkey economy as irrational as ours [3]

      I want to start with two observations about the human species. The first observation is something that you might think is quite obvious, and that's that our species, Homo sapiens, is actually really, really smart -- like, ridiculously smart -- like you're all doing things that no other species on the planet does right now. And this is, of course, not the first time you've probably recognized this. Of course, in addition to being smart, we're also an extremely vain species. So, we like pointing out the fact that we're smart. You know, so I could turn to pretty much any sage from Shakespeare to Stephen Colbert to point out things like the fact that we're noble in reason and infinite in faculties and just kind of awesome-er than anything else on the planet when it comes to all things cerebral.

)[3] Daniel Kahneman: Thinking, Fast and Slow. Amazon, 2013.

But of course, there's a second observation about the human species that I want to focus on a little bit more, and that's the fact that even though we're actually really smart, sometimes uniquely smart, we can also be incredibly, incredibly dumb when it comes to some aspects of our decision making. Now I'm seeing lots of smirks out there. Don't worry, I'm not going to call anyone in particular out on any aspects of your own mistakes. But of course, just in the last two years we see these unprecedented examples of human ineptitude. And we've watched as the tools we uniquely make to pull the resources out of our environment kind of just blow up in our face. We've watched the financial markets that we uniquely create -- these markets that were supposed to be foolproof -- we've watched them kind of collapse before our eyes.

But both of these two embarrassing examples, I think, don't highlight what I think is most embarrassing about the mistakes that humans make, which is that we'd like to think that the mistakes we make are really just the result of a couple bad apples or a couple really sort of FAIL Blog-worthy decisions. But it turns out, what social scientists are actually learning is that most of us, when put in certain contexts, will actually make very specific mistakes. The errors we make are actually predictable. We make them again and again. And they're actually immune to lots of evidence. When we get negative feedback, we still, the next time we're face with a certain context, tend to make the same errors. And so, this has been a real puzzle to me as a sort of scholar of human nature. What I'm most curious about is, how is a species that's as smart as we are capable of such bad and such consistent errors all the time?

You know, we're the smartest thing out there, why can't we figure this out? In some sense, where do our mistakes really come from? And having thought about this a little bit,

I see a couple different possibilities. One possibility is, in some sense, it's not really our fault. Because we're a smart species, we can actually create all kinds of environments that are super, super complicated, sometimes too complicated for us to even actually understand, even though we've actually created them. We create financial markets that are super complex. We create mortgage terms that we can't actually deal with. And of course, if we are put in environments where we can't deal with it, in some sense makes sense that we actually might mess certain things up. If this was the case, we'd have a really easy solution to the problem of human error. We'd actually just say, okay, let's figure out the kinds of technologies we can't deal with, the kinds of environments that are bad -- get rid of those, design things better, and we should be the noble species that we expect ourselves to be.

But there's another possibility that I find a little bit more worrying, which is, maybe it's not our environments that are messed up. Maybe it's actually us that's designed badly. This is a hint that I've gotten from watching the ways that social scientists have learned about human errors. And what we see is that people tend to keep making errors exactly the same way, over and over again. It feels like we might almost just be built to make errors in certain ways. This is a possibility that I worry a little bit more about, because, if it's us that's messed up, it's not actually clear how we go about dealing with it. We might just have to accept the fact that we're error prone and try to design things around it.

So, this is the question my students and I wanted to get at. How can we tell the difference between possibility one and possibility two? What we need is a population that's basically smart, can make lots of decisions, but doesn't have access to any of the systems we have, any of the things that might mess us up -- no human technology, human culture, maybe even not human language. And so this is why we turned to these guys here. These are one of the guys I work with. This is a brown capuchin monkey. These guys are New World primates, which means they broke off from the human branch about 35 million years ago. This means that your great, great, great great, great, great -- with about five million "greats" in their -- grandmother was probably the same great, great, great, great grandmother with five million "greats" in there as Holly up here. You know, so you can take comfort in the fact that this guy up here is a really distant, but albeit evolutionary, relative. The good news about Holly though is that she doesn't actually have the same kinds of technologies we do. You know, she's a smart, very cut creature, a primate as well, but she lacks all the stuff we think might be messing us up. So she's the perfect test case.

What if we put Holly into the same context as humans? Does she make the same mistakes as us? Does she not learn from them? And so on. And so, this is the kind of thing we decided to do. My students and I got very excited about this a few years ago. We said, all right, let's, you know, throw so problems at Holly, see if she messes these things up. First problem is just, well, where should we start? Because, you know, it's great for us, but bad for humans. We make a lot of mistakes in a lot of different contexts. You know, where are we actually going to start with this? And because we started this work around the time of the financial collapse, around the time when foreclosures were hitting the news, we said, hhmm, maybe we should actually start in the financial domain. Maybe we should look at monkey's economic decisions and try to see if they do the same kinds of dumb things that we do.

Of course, that's when we hit a sort second problem -- a little bit more methodological -- which is that, maybe you guys don't know, but monkeys don't actually use money. I know, you haven't met them. But this is why, you know, they're not in the queue behind you at the grocery store or the ATM -- you know, they don't do this stuff. So now we faced, you know, a little bit of a problem here. How are we actually going to ask monkeys about money if they don't actually use it? So, we said, well, maybe we should just, actually just suck it up and teach monkeys how to use money. So that's just what we did. What you're looking at over here is actually the first unit that I know of of non-human currency. We weren't very creative at the time we started these studies, so we just called it a token. But this is the unit of currency that we've taught our monkeys at Yale to actually use with humans, to actually buy different pieces of food. It doesn't look like much -- in fact, it isn't like much.

Like most of our money, it's just a piece of metal. As those of you who've taken currencies home from your trip know, once you get home, it's actually pretty useless. It was useless to the monkeys at first before they realized what they could do with it. When we first gave it to them in their enclosures, they actually kind of picked them up, looked at them. They were these kinds of weird things. But very quickly, the monkeys realized that they could actually hand these tokens over to different humans in the lab for some food. And so, you see one of our monkeys, Mayday, up here doing this. This is A and B are kind of the points where she's sort of a little bit curious about these things -- doesn't know. There's this waiting hand from a human experimenter, and Mayday quickly figures out, apparently the human wants this. Hands it over, and then gets some food. It turns out not just Mayday, all of our monkeys get good at trading tokens with human salesman. So here's just a quick video of what this looks like. Here's Mayday. She's going to be trading a token for some food and waiting happily and getting her food. Here's Felix, I think. He's our alpha male; he's a kind of big guy. But he too waits patiently, gets his food and goes on.

So, the monkeys get really good at this. They're surprisingly good at this with very little training. We just allowed them to pick this up on their own. The question is: is this anything like human money? Is this a market at all, or did we just do a weird psychologist's trick by getting monkeys to do something, looking smart, but not really being smart. And so, we said, well, what would the monkeys spontaneously do if this was really their currency, if they were really using it like money? Well, you might actually imagine them to do all the kinds of smart things that humans do when they start exchanging money with each other. You might have them start paying attention to price, paying attention to how much they buy -- sort of keeping track of their monkey token, as it were. Do the monkeys do anything like this?

And so, our monkey marketplace was born. The way this works is that our monkeys normally live in a kind of big zoo social enclosure. When they get a hankering for some treats, we actually allowed them a way out into a little smaller enclosure where they could enter the market. Upon entering the market -- it was actually a much more fun market for the monkeys than most human markets because, as the monkeys entered the door of the market, a human would give them a big wallet full of tokens so they could actually trade the tokens with one of these two guys here -- two different possible human salesmen that they could actually buy stuff from. The salesmen were students from my lab. They dressed differently; they were different people. And over time, they did basically the same thing so the monkeys could learn, you know, who sold what at what price -- you know, who was reliable, who wasn't, and so on. And you can see that each of the experimenters is actually holding up a little, yellow food dish. and that's what the monkey can for a single token. So, everything costs one token, but as you can see, sometimes tokens buy more than others, sometimes more grapes than others.

So, I'll show you a quick video of what this marketplace actually looks like. Here's a monkey-eye-view. Monkeys are shorter, so it's a little short. But here's Honey. She's waiting for the market to open a little impatiently. All of a sudden, the market opens. Here's her choice: one grape or two grapes. You can see Honey, very good market economist, goes with the guy who gives more. She could teach our financial advisers a few things or two. So not just Honey, most of the monkeys went with guys who had more. Most of the monkeys went with guys who had better food. When we introduced sales, we saw the monkeys paid attention to that. They really cared about their monkey token dollar. The more surprising thing was that when we collaborated with economists to actually look at the monkeys' data using economic tools, they basically matched, not just qualitatively, but quantitatively with what we saw humans doing in a real market. So much so that, if you saw the monkeys' numbers, you couldn't tell whether they came from a monkey or a human in the same market.

And what we'd really thought we'd done is like we'd actually introduced something that, at least for the monkeys and us, works like a real financial currency. Question is: do the monkeys start messing up in the same ways we do? Well, we already saw anecdotally a couple of signs that they might. One thing we never saw in the monkey marketplace was any evidence of saving -- you know, just like our own species. The monkeys entered the market, spent their entire budget and then went back to everyone else. The other thing we also spontaneously saw, embarrassingly enough, is spontaneous evidence of larceny. The monkeys would rip-off the tokens at every available opportunity -- from each other, often from us -- you know, things we didn't necessarily think we were introducing, but things we spontaneously saw.

So we said, this looks bad. Can we actually see if the monkeys are doing exactly the same dumb things as humans do? One possibility is just kind of let the monkey financial system play out, you know, see if they start calling us for bailouts in a few years. We were a little impatient so we wanted to sort of speed things up a bit. So we said, let's actually give the monkeys the same kinds of problems that humans tend to get wrong in certain kinds of economic challenges, or certain kinds of economic experiments. And so, since the best way to see how people go wrong is to actually do it yourself, I'm going to give you guys a quick experiment to sort of watch your own financial intuitions in action.

So, imagine that right now I handed each and every one of you a thousand U.S. dollars -- so 10 crisps hundred-dollar bills. Take these, put it in your wallet and spend a second thinking about what you're going to do with it. Because it's yours now; you can buy whatever you want. Donate it, take it, and so on. Sounds great, but you get one more choice to earn a little bit more money. And here's your choice: you can either be risky, in which case I'm going to flip one of these monkey tokens. If it comes up heads, you're going to get a thousand dollars more. If it comes up tails, you get nothing. So it's a chance to get more, but it's pretty risky. Your other option is a bit safe. You're just going to get some money for sure. I'm just going to give you 500 bucks. You can stick it in your wallet and use it immediately. So, see what your intuition is here. Most people actually go with the play-it-safe option. Most people say, why should I be risky when I can get 1,500 dollars for sure? This seems like a good bet. I'm going to go with that. You might say, eh, that's not really irrational. People are a little risk-averse. So what?

Well, the "so what?" comes when start thinking about the same problem set up just a little bit differently. So now imagine that I give each and every one of you 2,000 dollars -- 20 crisp hundred-dollar bills. Now you can buy double to stuff you were going to get before. Think about how you'd feel sticking it in your wallet. And now imagine that I have you make another choice but this time, it's a little bit worse. Now, you're going to be deciding how you're going to lose money, but you're going to get the same choice. You can either take a risky loss -- so I'll flip a coin. If it comes up heads, you're going to actually lose a lot. If it comes up tails, you lose nothing, you're fine, get to keep the whole thing -- or you could play it safe, which means you have to reach back into your wallet and give me five of those $100 bills, for certain.

And I'm seeing a lot of furrowed brows out there. So maybe you're having the same intuitions as the subjects that were actually tested in this, which is when presented with these options, people don't choose to play it safe. They actually tend to go a little risky. The reason this is irrational is that we've given people in both situations the same choice. It's a 50/50 shot of a thousand or 2,000, or just 1,500 dollars with certainty. But people's intuitions about how much risk to take varies depending on where they started with.

So, what's going on? Well, it turns out that this seems to be the result of at least two biases that we have at the psychological level. One is that we have a really hard time thinking in absolute terms. You really have to do work to figure out, well, one option's a thousand, 2,000; one is 1,500. Instead, we find it very easy to think in very relative terms as options change from one time to another. So, we think of things as, "Oh, I'm going to get more," or "Oh, I'm going to get less." This is all well and good, except that changes in different directions actually effect whether or not we think options are good or not. And this leads to the second bias, which economists have called loss aversion.

The idea is that we really hate it when things go into the red. We really hate it when we have to lose out on some money. And this means that sometimes we'll actually switch our preferences to avoid this. What you saw in that last scenario is that subjects get risky because they want the small shot that there won't be any loss. That means when we're in a risk mindset -- excuse me, when we're in a loss mindset, we actually become riskier, which can actually be really worrying. These kinds of things play out in lots of bad ways in humans. They're why stock investors hold onto losing stocks longer --

because they're evaluating them in relative terms. They're why people in the housing market refused to sell their house -- because they don't want to sell at a loss.

The question we were interested in is whether the monkeys show the same biases. If we set up those same scenarios in our little monkey market, would they do the same thing as people? And so this is what we did, we gave the monkeys choices between guys who were safe -- they did the same thing every time -- or guys who were risky -- they did things differently half the time. And then we gave them options that were bonuses -- like you guys did in the first scenario -- so they actually have a chance more, or pieces where they were experiencing losses -- they actually thought they were going to get more than they really got.

And so, this is what this looks like. We introduced the monkeys to two new monkey salesmen. The guy on the left and right both start with one piece of grape, so it looks pretty good. But they're going to give the monkeys bonuses. The guy on the left is a safe bonus. All the time, he adds one, to give the monkeys two. The guy on the right is actually a risky bonus. Sometimes the monkeys get no bonus -- so this is a bonus of zero. Sometimes the monkeys get two extras. For a big bonus, now they get three. But this is the same choice you guys just faced. Do the monkeys actually want to play it safe and then go with the guy who's going to do the same thing on every trial, or do they want to be risky and try to get a risky, but big, bonus, but risk the possibility of getting no bonus. People here played it safe. Turns out, the monkeys play it safe too. Qualitatively and quantitatively, they choose exactly the same way as people, when tested in the same thing.

You might say, well, maybe the monkeys just don't like risk. Maybe we should see how they do with losses. And so, we ran a second version of this. Now, the monkeys meet two guys who aren't giving them bonuses; they're actually giving them less than they expect. So they look like they're starting out with a big amount. These are three grapes; the monkeys really psyched for this. But now they learn these guys are going to give them less than they expect. They guy on the left is a safe loss. Every single time, he's going to take one of these away and give the monkeys just two. the guy on the right is the risky loss. Sometimes he gives no loss, so the monkeys are really psyched, but sometimes he actually gives a big loss, taking away two to give the monkeys only one.

And so, what do the monkeys do? Again, same choice; they can play it safe for always getting two grapes every single time, or they can take a risky bet and choose between one and three. The remarkable thing to us is that, when you give monkeys this choice, they do the same irrational thing that people do. They actually become riskier depending on how the experimenters started. This is crazy because it suggests that the monkeys too are evaluating things in relative terms and actually treating losses differently than they treat gains.

So, what does all of this mean? Well, what we've shown is that, first of all, we can actually give the monkeys a financial currency, and they do very similar things with it. They do some of the smart things we do, some of the kind of not so nice things we do, like steal it and so on. But they also do some of the irrational things we do. They systematically get things wrong and in the same ways that we do. This is the first take-home message of the Talk, which is that if you saw the beginning of this and you thought, oh, I'm totally going to go home and hire a capuchin monkey financial adviser. They're way cuter than the one at ... you know -- Don't do that; they're probably going to be just as dumb as the human one you already have. So, you know, a little bad -- Sorry, sorry, sorry. A little bad for monkey investors.

But of course, you know, the reason you're laughing is bad for humans too. Because we've answered the question we started out with. We wanted to know where these kinds of errors came from. And we started with the hope that maybe we can sort of tweak our financial institutions, tweak our technologies to make ourselves better. But what we've learn is that these biases might be a deeper part of us than that. In fact, they might be due to the very nature of our evolutionary history. You know, maybe it's not just humans at the right side of this chain that's duncey. Maybe it's sort of duncey all the way back. And this, if we believe the capuchin monkey results, means that these duncey strategies might be 35 million years old. That's a long time for a strategy to potentially get changed around -- really, really old.

What do we know about other old strategies like this? Well, one thing we know is that they tend to be really hard to overcome. You know, think of our evolutionary predilection for eating sweet things, fatty things like cheesecake. You can't just shut that off. You can't just look at the dessert cart as say, "No, no, no. That looks disgusting to me." We're just built differently. We're going to perceive it as a good thing to go after. My guess is that the same thing is going to be true when humans are perceiving different financial decisions. When you're watching your stocks plummet into the red, when you're watching your house price go down, you're not going to be able to see that in anything but old evolutionary terms. This means that the biases that lead investors to do badly, that lead to the foreclosure crisis are going to be really hard to overcome.

So that's the bad news. The question is: is there any good news? I'm supposed to be up here telling you the good news. Well, the good news, I think, is what I started with at the beginning of the Talk, which is that humans are not only smart; we're really inspirationally smart to the rest of the animals in the biological kingdom. We're so good at overcoming our biological limitations -- you know, I flew over here in an airplane. I didn't have to try to flap my wings. I'm wearing contact lenses now so that I can see all of you. I don't have to rely on my own near-sightedness. We actually have all of these cases where we overcome our biological limitations through technology and other means, seemingly pretty easily. But we have to recognize that we have those limitations.

And here's the rub. It was Camus who once said that, "Man is the only species who refuses to be what he really is." But the irony is that it might only be in recognizing our limitations that we can really actually overcome them. The hope is that you all will think about

52

your limitations, not necessarily as unovercomable, but to recognize them, accept them and then use the world of design to actually figure them out. That might be the only way that we will really be able to achieve our own human potential and really be the noble species we hope to all be.

Chapter 4
The battle between your present and future self [4]

Do you remember the story of Odysseus and the Sirens from high school or junior high school? There was this hero, Odysseus, who's heading back home after the Trojan War. And he's standing on the deck of his ship, he's talking to his first mate, and he's saying, "Tomorrow, we will sail past those rocks, and on those rocks sit some beautiful women called Sirens. And these women sing an enchanting song, a song so alluring that all sailors who hear it crash into the rocks and die." Now you would expect, given that, that they would choose an alternate route around the Sirens, but instead Odysseus says, "I want to hear that song. And so what I'm going to do is I'm going to pour wax in the ears of you and all the men -- stay with me -- so that you can't hear the song, and then I'm going to have you tie me to the mast so that I can listen and we can all

)[4] Daniel goldstiein: behavioral economist.

sail by unaffected." So, this is a captain putting the life of every single person on the ship at risk so that he can hear a song.

And I'd like to think if this was the case, they probably would have rehearsed it a few times. Odysseus would have said, "Okay, let's do a dry run. You tie me to the mast, and I'm going to beg and plead. And no matter what I say, you cannot untie me from the mast. All right, so tie me to the mast." And the first mate takes a rope and ties Odysseus to the mast in a nice knot. And Odysseus does his best job playacting and says, "Untie me. Untie me. I want to hear that song. Untie me." And the first mate wisely resists and doesn't untie Odysseus. And then Odysseus says, "I see that you can get it. All right, untie me now and we'll get some dinner." And the first mate hesitates. He's like, "Is this still the rehearsal, or should I untie him?" And the first mate thinks, "Well, I guess at some point the rehearsal has to end." So, he unties Odysseus, and Odysseus flips out. He's like, "You idiot. You moron. If you do that tomorrow, I'll be dead, you'll be dead, every single one of the men will be dead. Now just don't untie me no matter what." He throws the first mate to the ground. This repeats itself through the night -- rehearsal, tying to the mast, conning his way out of it, beating the poor first mate up mercilessly. Hilarity ensues.

Tying yourself to a mast is perhaps the oldest written example of what psychologists call a commitment device. A commitment device is a decision that you make with a cool head to bind yourself so that you don't do something regrettable when you have a hot head. Because there's two heads inside one person when you think about it. Scholars have long invoked this metaphor of two selves when it comes to questions of temptation. There is first, the present self. This is like Odysseus when he's hearing the song. He just wants to get to the front row. He just thinks about the here and now and the immediate gratification. But then there's this other self, the future self. This is Odysseus as an old man who wants nothing more than to retire in a sunny villa with his wife Penelope outside of Ithaca -- the other one.

So why do we need commitment devices? Well resisting temptation is hard, as the 19th century English economist Nassau William Senior said, "To abstain from the enjoyment which is in our power, or to seek distant rather than immediate results, are among the most painful exertions of the human will." If you set goals for yourself and you're like a lot of other people, you probably realize it's not that your goals are physically impossible that's keeping you from achieving them, it's that you lack the self-discipline to stick to them. It's physically possible to lose weight. It's physically possible to exercise more. But resisting temptation is hard.

The other reason that it's difficult to resist temptation is because it's an unequal battle between the present self and the future self. I mean, let's face it, the present self is present. It's in control. It's in power right now. It has these strong, heroic arms that can lift doughnuts into your mouth. And the future self is not even around. It's off in the future. It's weak. It doesn't even have a lawyer present. There's nobody to stick up for the future self. And so, the present self can trounce all over its dreams. So, there's this battle between the two selves that's being fought, and we need commitment devices to level the playing field between the two.

Now I'm a big fan of commitment devices actually. Tying yourself to the mast is the oldest one, but there are other ones such as locking a credit card away with a key or not bringing junk food into the house so you won't eat it or unplugging your Internet connection so you can use your computer. I was creating commitment devices of my own long before I knew what they were. So, when I was a starving post-doc at Columbia University, I was deep in a publish-or-perish phase of my career. I had to write five pages a day towards papers or I would have to give up five dollars.

And when you try to execute these commitment devices, you realize the devil is really in the details. Because it's not that easy to get rid of five dollars. I mean, you can't burn it; that's illegal. And I thought, well I could give it to a charity or give it to my wife or something like that. But then I thought, oh, I'm sending myself mixed messages. Because not writing is bad, but giving to charity is good. So then I would kind of justify not writing by giving a gift. And then I kind of flipped that around and thought, well I could give it to the neo-Nazis. But then I was like, that's worse than writing is good, and so that wouldn't work. So ultimately, I just decided I would leave it in an envelope on the subway. Sometimes a good person would find it, sometimes a bad person would find it. On average, it was just a completely pointless exchange of money that I would regret. Such it is with commitment devices.

But despite my like for them, there's two nagging concerns that I've always had about commitment devices, and you might feel this if you use them yourself. So, the first is, when you've got one of these devices going, such as this contract to write every day or pay, it's just a constant reminder that you have no self-control. You're just telling yourself, "Without you, commitment device, I am nothing, I have no self-discipline." And then when you're ever in a situation where you don't have a commitment device in place -- like, "Oh my God, that person's offering me a doughnut, and I have no defense mechanism," -- you just eat it. So, I don't like the way that they take the power away from you. I think self-discipline is something, it's like a muscle. The more you exercise it, the stronger it gets.

The other problem with commitment devices is that you can always weasel your way out of them. You say, "Well, of course I can't write today, because I have five media interviews, and then I'm going to a cocktail party and then I'll be drunk after that. And so, there's no way that this is going to work." So, in effect, you are like Odysseus and the first mate in one person. You're putting yourself; you're binding yourself, and you're weaseling your way out of it, and then you're beating yourself up afterwards.

So, I've been working for about a decade now on finding other ways to change people's relationship to the future self without using commitment devices. In particular, I'm interested in the relationship to the future financial self. And this is a timely issue. I'm talking about the topic of saving. Now saving is a classic two selves problem. The present self does not want to save at all. It wants to consume. Whereas the future self wants the present self to save. So, this is a timely problem. We look at the savings rate and it has been declining since the 1950s. At the same time, the Retirement Risk Index, the chance of not being able to meet your needs in retirement, has been increasing. And we're at a situation now where for every three baby boomers, the McKinsey Global Institute predicts that two will not be able to meet their pre-retirement needs while they're in retirement.

So, what can we do about this? There's a philosopher, Derek Parfit, who said some words that were inspiring to my coauthors and I. He said that, "We might neglect our future selves because of some failure of belief or imagination." That is to say, we somehow might not believe that we're going to get old, or we might not be able to imagine that we're going to get old someday. On the one hand, it sounds ridiculous. Of course, we know that we're going to get old. But aren't there things that we believe and don't believe at the same time?

So, my coauthors and I have used computers, the greatest tool of our time, to assist people's imagination and help them imagine what it might be like to go into the future. And I'll show you some of these tools right here. The first is called the distribution builder. It shows people what the future might be like by showing them a hundred equally probable outcomes that might be obtained in the future. Each outcome is shown by one of these markers, and each sit on a row that represents a level of wealth and retirement. Being up at the top means that you're enjoying a high income in retirement. Being down at the bottom means that you're struggling to make ends meet. When you make an investment, what you're really saying is, "I accept that any one of these 100 things could happen to me and determine my wealth."

Now you can try to move your outcomes around. You can try to manipulate your fate, like this person is doing, but it costs you something to do it. It means that you have to save more today. Once you find an investment that you're happy with, what people do is they click "done" and the markers begin to disappear, slowly, one by one. It simulates what it is like to invest in something and to watch that investment pan out. At the end, there will only be one marker left standing and it will determine our wealth in retirement.

Yes, this person retired at 150 percent of their working income in retirement. They're making more money while retired than they were making while they were working. If you're like most people, just seeing that gave you a small sense of elation and joy -- just to think about making 50 percent more money in retirement than before. However, had you ended up on the very bottom, it might have given you a slight sense of dread and/or nausea thinking about struggling to get by in retirement. By using this tool over and over and simulating outcome after outcome, people can understand that the investments and savings that they undertake today determine their well-being in the future.

Now people are motivated through emotions, but different people find different things motivating. This is a simulation that uses graphics, but other people find motivating what money can buy, not just numbers. So here I made a distribution builder where instead of showing numerical outcomes, I show people what those outcomes will get you, in particular apartments that you can afford if you're retiring on 3,000, 2,500, 2,000 dollars per month and so on. As you move down the ladder of apartments, you see that they get worse and worse. Some of them look like places I lived in as a graduate student. And as you get to the very bottom, you're faced with the unfortunate reality that if you don't save anything for retirement, you won't be able to afford any housing at all. Those are actual pictures of actual apartments renting for that amount as advertised on the Internet.

The last thing I'll show you, the last behavioral time machine, is something that I created with Hal Hershfield, who was introduced to me by my coauthor on a previous project, Bill Sharpe. And what it is an exploration into virtual reality. So, what we do is we take pictures of people -- in this case, college-age people -- and we use software to age them and show these people what they'll look like when they're 60, 70, 80 years old. And we try to test whether actually assisting your imagination by looking at the face of your future self can change your investment behavior.

So, this is one of our experiments. Here we see the face of the young subject on the left. He's given a control that allows him to adjust his savings rate. As he moves his savings rate down, it means that he's saving zero when it's all the way here at the left. You can see his current annual income -- this is the percentage of his paycheck that he can take home today -- is quite high, 91 percent, but his retirement income is quite low. He's going to retire on 44 percent of what he earned while he was working. If he saves the maximum legal amount, his retirement income goes up, but he's unhappy because now he has less money on the left-hand side to spend today. Other conditions show people the future self. And from the future self's point of view, everything is in reverse. If you save very little, the future self is unhappy living on 44 percent of the income. Whereas if the present self-saves a lot, the future self is delighted, where the income is close up near 100 percent.

To bring this to a wider audience, I've been working with Hal and Allianz to create something we call the behavioral time machine, in which you not only get to see yourself in the future, but you get to see anticipated emotional reactions to different levels of retirement wealth. So, for instance, here is somebody using the tool. And just watch the facial expressions as they move the slider. The younger face gets happier and happier, saving nothing. The older face is miserable. And slowly, slowly we're bringing it up to a moderate savings rate. And then it's a high savings rate. The younger face is getting unhappy. The older face is quite pleased with the decision. We're going to see if this has an effect on what people do. And what's nice about it is it's not something that biasing people actually, because as one face smiles, the other face frowns. It's not telling you which way to put the slider, it's just reminding you that you are connected to and legally tied to this future self.

Your decisions today are going to determine its well-being. And that's something that's easy to forget. This use of virtual reality is not just good for making people look older. There are programs you can get to see how people might look if they smoke, if they get too much exposure to the sun, if they gain weight and so on. And what's good is, unlike in the experiments that Hal and myself ran with Russ Smith, you don't have to program these by yourself in order to see the virtual reality. There are applications you can get on smartphones for just a few dollars that do the same thing. This is actually a picture of Hal, my coauthor. You might recognize him from the previous demos. And just for kicks we ran his picture through the balding, aging and weight gain software to see how he would look. Hal is here, so I think we owe it to him as well as yourself to disabuse you of that last image. And I'll close it there.

Chapter 5
Saving for tomorrow [5]

I'm going to talk about Save More Tomorrow. It's a program that Richard Thaler from the University of Chicago and I devised maybe 15 years ago. The program, in a sense, is an example of behavioral finance on steroids -- how we could really use behavioral finance. Now you might ask, what is behavioral finance? So, let's think about how we manage our money. Let's start with mortgages. It's kind of a recent topic, at least in the U.S. A lot of people buy the biggest house they can afford, and actually slightly bigger than that. And then they foreclose. And then they blame the banks for being the bad guys who gave them the mortgages.

Let's also think about how we manage risks -- for example, investing in the stock market. Two years ago, three years ago, about four years ago, markets did well. We were risk

---

)[5] shlomo benartzi: economist.

takers, of course. Then market stocks seize and we're like, "Wow. These losses, they feel, emotionally, they feel very different from what we actually thought about it when markets were going up." So, we're probably not doing a great job when it comes to risk taking.

How many of you have iPhones? I would bet many more of you ensure your iPhone -- you're implicitly buying insurance by having an extended warranty. What if you lose your iPhone? What if you do this? How many of you have kids? I would predict, if you're a representative sample, that many more of you ensure your iPhones than your lives, even when you have kids. We're not doing that well when it comes to insurance.

The average American household spends 1,000 dollars a year on lotteries. And I know it sounds crazy. How many of you spend a thousand dollars a year on lotteries? No one. So that tells us that the people not in this room are spending more than a thousand to get the average to a thousand. Low-income people spend a lot more than a thousand on lotteries. So, where does it take us? We're not doing a great job managing money.

Behavioral finance is really a combination of psychology and economics, trying to understand the money mistakes people make. And I can keep standing here for the 12 minutes and 53 seconds that I have left and make fun of all sorts of ways we manage money, and at the end you're going to ask, "How can we help people?" And that's what I really want to focus on today. How do we take an understanding of the money mistakes people make, and then turning the behavioral challenges into behavioral solutions? And what I'm going to talk about today is Save More Tomorrow.

I want to address the issue of savings. We have on the screen a representative sample of 100 Americans. And we're going to look at their saving behavior. First thing to notice is, half of them do not even have access to a 401(k) plan. They cannot make savings easy. They cannot have money go away from their paycheck into a 401(k) plan before they see it, before they can touch it. What about the remaining half of the people? Some of them elect not to save. They're just too lazy. They never get around to logging into a complicated website and doing 17 clicks to join the 401(k) plan. And then they have to decide how they're going to invest in their 52 choices, and they never heard about what is a money market fund. And they get overwhelmed and the just don't join. How many people end up saving to a 401(k) plan? One third of Americans. Two thirds are not saving now.

Are they saving enough? Take out those who say they save too little. One out of 10 are saving enough. Nine out of 10 either cannot save through their 401(k) plan, decide not to save -- or don't decide -- or save too little. We think we have a problem of people saving too much. Let's look at that. We have one person -- well, actually we're going to slice him in half because it's less than one percent. Roughly half a percent of Americans feel that they save too much.

What are we going to do about it? That's what I really want to focus on. We have to understand why people are not saving, and then we can hopefully flip the behavioral challenges into behavioral solutions, and then see how powerful it might be. So, let me divert for a second as we're going to identify the problems, the challenges, the behavioral challenges, that prevent people from saving. I'm going to divert and talk about bananas and chocolate.

Suppose we had an event next week. And during the break there would be a snack and you could choose bananas or chocolate. How many of you think you would like to have bananas during this hypothetical event next week? Who would go for bananas? I predict scientifically 74 percent of you will go for bananas. Well that's at least what one wonderful study predicted. And then count down the days and see what people ended up eating. The same people that imagined themselves eating the bananas ended up eating chocolates a week later.

Self-control is not a problem in the future. It's only a problem now when the chocolate is next to us. What does it have to do with time and savings, this issue of immediate gratification? Or as some economists call it, present bias. We think about saving.

We know we should be saving. We know we'll do it next year, but today let us go and spend. Christmas is coming, we might as well buy a lot of gifts for everyone we know. So, this issue of present bias causes us to think about saving, but end up spending.

Let me now talk about another behavioral obstacle to saving having to do with inertia. But again, a little diversion to the topic of organ donation. Wonderful study comparing different countries. We're going to look at two similar countries, Germany and Austria. And in Germany, if you would like to donate your organs -- God forbid something really bad happens to you -- when you get your driving license or an I.D., you check the box saying, "I would like to donate my organs." Not many people like checking boxes.

It takes effort. You need to think. Twelve percent do. Austria, a neighboring country, slightly similar, slightly different. What's the difference? Well, you still have choice. You will decide whether you want to donate your organs or not. But when you get your driving license, you check the box if you do not want to donate your organ. Nobody checks boxes. That's kind of too much effort. One percent check the box. The rest do nothing. Doing nothing is very common. Not many people check boxes.

What are the implications to saving lives and having organs available? In Germany, 12 percent check the box. Twelve percent are organ donors. Huge shortage of organs, God forbid, if you need one. In Austria, again, nobody checks the box.

Therefore, 99 percent of people are organ donors. Inertia, lack of action. What is the default setting if people do nothing, if they keep procrastinating, if they don't check the boxes? Very powerful. We're going to talk about what happens if people are overwhelmed and scared to make their 401(k) choices. Are we going to make them automatically join the plan, or are they going to be left out? In too many 401(k) plans, if people do nothing, it means they're not saving for retirement, if they don't check the box. And checking the box takes effort.

So, we've chatted about a couple of behavioral challenges. One more before we flip the challenges into solutions, having to do with monkeys and apples. No, no, no, this is a real study and it's got a lot to do with behavioral economics. One group of monkeys gets an apple, they're pretty happy. The other group gets two apples, one is taken away. They still have an apple left. They're really mad. Why have you taken our apple? This is the notion of loss aversion.

We hate losing stuff, even if it doesn't mean a lot of risk. You would hate to go to the ATM, take out 100 dollars and notice that you lost one of those $20 bills. It's very painful, even though it doesn't mean anything. Those 20 dollars might have been a quick lunch. So this notion of loss aversion kicks in when it comes to savings too, because people, mentally and emotionally and intuitively frame savings as a loss because I have to cut my spending.

So, we talked about all sorts of behavioral challenges having to do with savings eventually. Whether you think about immediate gratification, and the chocolates versus bananas, it's just painful to save now. It's a lot more fun to spend now. We talked about inertia and organ donations and checking the box. If people have to check a lot of boxes to join a 401(k) plan, they're going to keep procrastinating and not join. And last, we talked about loss aversion, and the monkeys and the apples. If people frame mentally saving for retirement as a loss, they're not going to be saving for retirement.

So, we've got these challenges, and what Richard Thaler and I were always fascinated by -- take behavioral finance, make it behavioral finance on steroids or behavioral finance 2.0 or behavioral finance in action -- flip the challenges into solutions. And we came up with an embarrassingly simple solution called Save More, not today, Tomorrow. How is it going to solve the challenges we chatted about? If you think about the problem of bananas versus chocolates, we think we're going to eat bananas next week.

We think we're going to save more next year. Save More Tomorrow invites employees to save more maybe next year -- sometime in the future when we can imagine ourselves eating bananas, volunteering more in the community, exercising more and doing all the right things on the planet.

Now we also talked about checking the box and the difficulty of taking action. Save More Tomorrow makes it easy. It's an autopilot.

Once you tell me you would like to save more in the future, let's say every January you're going to be saving more automatically and it's going to go away from your paycheck to the 401(k) plan before you see it, before you touch it, before you get the issue of immediate gratification. But what are we going to do about the monkeys and loss aversion? Next January comes and people might feel that if they save more, they have to spend less, and that's painful. Well, maybe it shouldn't be just January. Maybe we should make people save more when they make more money.

That way, when they make more money, when they get a pay raise, they don't have to cut their spending. They take a little bit of the increase in the paycheck home and spend more -- take a little bit of the increase and put it in a 401(k) plan.

So that is the program, embarrassingly simple, but as we're going to see, extremely powerful. We first implemented it, Richard Thaler and I, back in 1998. Mid-sized company in the Midwest, blue collar employees struggling to pay their bills repeatedly told us they cannot save more right away.

Saving more today is not an option. We invited them to save three percentage points more every time they get a pay raise. And here are the results. We're seeing here a three and a half-year period, four pay raises, people who were struggling to save, were saving three percent of their paycheck, three and a half years later saving almost four times as much, almost 14 percent.

And there's shoes and bicycles and things on this chart because I don't want to just throw numbers in a vacuum. I want, really, to think about the fact that saving four times more is a huge difference in terms of the lifestyle that people will be able to afford. It's real. It's not just numbers on a piece of paper. Whereas with saving three percent, people might have to add nice sneakers so they can walk, because they won't be able to afford anything else, when they save 14 percent, they might be able to maybe have nice dress shoes to walk to the car to drive.

This is a real difference. By now, about 60 percent of the large companies actually have programs like this in place. It's been part of the Pension Protection Act. And needless to say, that Thaler and I have been blessed to be part of this program and make a difference.

Let me wrap with two key messages. One is behavioral finance is extremely powerful. This is just one example. Message two is there's still a lot to do. This is really the tip of the iceberg. If you think about people and mortgages and buying houses and then not being able to pay for it, we need to think about that. If you're thinking about people taking too much risk and not understanding how much risk they're taking or taking too little risk, we need to think about that. If you think about people spending a thousand dollars a year on lottery tickets, we need to think about that. The average actually, the record is in Singapore. The average household spends $4,000 a year on lottery tickets. We've got a lot to do, a lot to solve, also in the retirement area when it comes to what people do with their money after retirement.

One last question: How many of you feel comfortable that as you're planning for retirement you have a really solid plan when you're going to retire, when you're going to claim Social Security benefits, what lifestyle to expect, how much to spend every month so you're not going to run out of money? How many of you feel you have a solid plan for the future when it comes to post-retirement decisions? One, two, three, four. Less than three percent of a very sophisticated audience. Behavioral finance has a long way. There's a lot of opportunities to make it powerful again and again and again.

Chapter 6
Could your language affect your ability to save money? [6]

The global economic financial crisis has reignited public interest in something that's actually one of the oldest questions in economics, dating back to at least before Adam Smith. And that is, why is it that countries with seemingly similar economies and institutions can display radically different savings behavior?

Now, many brilliant economists have spent their entire lives working on this question, and as a field we've made a tremendous amount of headway and we understand a lot about this. What I'm here to talk with you about today is an intriguing new hypothesis and some surprisingly powerful new findings that I've been working on about the link between the structure of the language you speak and how you find yourself with the

_____

[6] keith chen: behavioral economist.

propensity to save. Let me tell you a little bit about savings rates, a little bit about language, and then I'll draw that connection.

Let's start by thinking about the member countries of the OECD, or the Organization of Economic Cooperation and Development. OECD countries, by and large, you should think about these as the richest, most industrialized countries in the world. And by joining the OECD, they were affirming a common commitment to democracy, open markets and free trade. Despite all of these similarities, we see huge differences in savings behavior.

So, all the way over on the left of this graph, what you see is many OECD countries saving over a quarter of their GDP every year, and some OECD countries saving over a third of their GDP per year. Holding down the right flank of the OECD, all the way on the other side, is Greece. And what you can see is that over the last 25 years, Greece has barely managed to save more than 10 percent of their GDP. It should be noted, of course, that the United States and the U.K. are the next in line.

Now that we see these huge differences in savings rates, how is it possible that language might have something to do with these differences? Let me tell you a little bit about how languages fundamentally differ. Linguists and cognitive scientists have been exploring this question for many years now. And then I'll draw the connection between these two behaviors.

I grew up in the Midwest of the United States. And something I realized quite early on was that the Chinese language forced me to speak about and -- in fact, more fundamentally than that -- ever so slightly forced me to think about family in very different ways.

Now, how might that be? Let me give you an example. Suppose I were talking with you and I was introducing you to my uncle. You understood exactly what I just said in English. If we were speaking Mandarin

Chinese with each other, though, I wouldn't have that luxury. I wouldn't have been able to convey so little information. What my language would have forced me to do, instead of just telling you, "This is my uncle," is to tell you a tremendous amount of additional information. My language would force me to tell you whether or not this was an uncle on my mother's side or my father's side, whether this was an uncle by marriage or by birth, and if this man was my father's brother, whether he was older than or younger than my father. All of this information is obligatory. Chinese doesn't let me ignore it. And in fact, if I want to speak correctly, Chinese forces me to constantly think about it.

Now, that fascinated me endlessly as a child, but what fascinates me even more today as an economist is that some of these same differences carry through to how languages speak about time. So, for example, if I'm speaking in English, I have to speak grammatically differently if I'm talking about past rain, "It rained yesterday," current rain, "It is raining now," or future rain, "It will rain tomorrow." Notice that English requires a lot more information with respect to the timing of events. Why? Because I have to consider that and I have to modify what I'm saying to say, "It will rain," or "It's going to rain." It's simply not permissible in English to say, "It rain tomorrow."

In contrast to that, that's almost exactly what you would say in Chinese. A Chinese speaker can basically say something that sounds very strange to an English speaker's ears. They can say, "Yesterday it rain," "Now it rain," "Tomorrow it rain." In some deep sense, Chinese doesn't divide up the time spectrum in the same way that English forces us to constantly do in order to speak correctly.

Is this difference in languages only between very, very distantly related languages, like English and Chinese? Actually, no. So many of you know, in this room, that English is a Germanic language. What you may not have realized is that English is actually an outlier. It is the only Germanic language that requires this. For example, most other Germanic language speakers feel completely comfortable talking about rain tomorrow by saying, "Morgen regnet es," quite literally to an English ear, "It rain tomorrow."

This led me, as a behavioral economist, to an intriguing hypothesis. Could how you speak about time, could how your language forces you to think about time, affect your propensity to behave across time? You speak English, a futured language. And what that means is that every time you discuss the future, or any kind of a future event, grammatically you're forced to cleave that from the present and treat it as if it's something viscerally different. Now suppose that that visceral difference makes you subtly dissociate the future from the present every time

90

you speak. If that's true and it makes the future feel like something more distant and more different from the present, that's going to make it harder to save. If, on the other hand, you speak a futureless language, the present and the future, you speak about them identically. If that subtly nudges you to feel about them identically, that's going to make it easier to save.

Now this is a fanciful theory. I'm a professor, I get paid to have fanciful theories. But how would you actually go about testing such a theory? Well, what I did with that was to access the linguistics literature. And interestingly enough, there are pockets of futureless language speakers situated all over the world. This is a pocket of futureless language speakers in Northern Europe. Interestingly enough, when you start to crank the data, these pockets of futureless language speakers all around the world turn out to be, by and large, some of the world's best savers.

Just to give you a hint of that, let's look back at that OECD graph that we were talking about. What you see is that these bars are systematically taller and systematically shifted to the left compared to these bars which are the members of the OECD that speak futured languages. What is the average difference here? Five percentage points of your GDP saved per year. Over 25 years that has huge long-run effects on the wealth of your nation.

Now while these findings are suggestive, countries can be different in so many different ways that it's very, very difficult sometimes to account for all of these possible differences. What I'm going to show you, though, is something that I've been engaging in for a year, which is trying to gather all of the largest datasets that we have access to as economists, and I'm going to try and strip away all of those possible differences, hoping to get this relationship to break. And just in summary, no matter how far I push this, I can't get it to break. Let me show you how far you can do that.

One way to imagine that is I gather large datasets from around the world. So, for example, there is the Survey of Health, [Aging] and Retirement in Europe. From this dataset you actually learn that retired European families are extremely patient with survey takers. So imagine that you're a retired household in Belgium and someone comes to your front door. "Excuse me, would you mind if I peruse your stock portfolio? Do you happen to know how much your house is worth? Do you mind telling me? Would you happen to have a hallway that's more than 10 meters long? If you do, would you mind if I timed how long it took you to walk down that hallway? Would you mind squeezing as hard as you can, in your dominant hand, this device so I can measure your grip strength? How about blowing into this tube so I can measure your lung capacity?" The survey takes over a day. Combine that with a Demographic and Health Survey collected by USAID in developing countries in Africa, for example, which that survey actually can go so far as to directly measure the HIV status of families living in, for example, rural Nigeria. Combine that with a world value survey, which measures the political opinions and, fortunately for me, the savings behaviors of millions of families in hundreds of countries around the world.

Take all of that data, combine it, and this map is what you get. What you find is nine countries around the world that have significant native populations which speak both futureless and futured languages. And what I'm going to do is form statistical matched pairs between families that are nearly identical on every dimension that I can measure, and then I'm going to explore whether or not the link between language and savings holds even after controlling for all of these levels.

What are the characteristics we can control for? Well I'm going to match families on country of birth and residence, the demographics -- what sex, their age -- their income level within their own country, their educational achievement, a lot about their family structure. It turns out there are six different ways to be married in Europe. And most granularly, I break them down by religion where there are 72 categories of religions in the world -- so an extreme level of granularity. There are 1.4 billion different ways that a family can find itself.

Now effectively everything I'm going to tell you from now on is only comparing these basically nearly identical families. It's getting as close as possible to the thought experiment of finding two families both of whom live in Brussels who are identical on every single one of these dimensions, but one of whom speaks

Flemish and one of whom speaks French; or two families that live in a rural district in Nigeria, one of whom speaks Hausa and one of whom speaks Igbo.

Now even after all of this granular level of control, do futureless language speakers seem to save more? Yes, futureless language speakers, even after this level of control, are 30 percent more likely to report having saved in any given year. Does this have cumulative effects? Yes, by the time they retire, futureless language speakers, holding constant their income, are going to retire with 25 percent more in savings.

Can we push this data even further? Yes, because I just told you, we actually collect a lot of health data as economists. Now how can we think about health behaviors to think about savings? Well, think about smoking, for example. Smoking is in some deep sense negative savings. If savings is current pain in exchange for future pleasure, smoking is just the opposite. It's current pleasure in exchange for future pain. What we should expect then is the opposite effect. And that's exactly what we find. Futureless language speakers are 20 to 24 percent less likely to be smoking at any given point in time compared to identical families, and they're going to be 13 to 17 percent less likely to be obese by the time they retire, and they're going to report being 21 percent more likely to have used a condom in their last sexual encounter. I could go on and on with the list of differences that you can find. It's almost impossible not to find a savings behavior for which this strong effect isn't present.

My linguistics and economics colleagues at Yale and I are just starting to do this work and really explore and understand the ways that these subtle nudges cause us to think more or less about the future every single time we speak. Ultimately, the goal, once we understand how these subtle effects can change our decision making, we want to be able to provide people tools so that they can consciously make themselves better savers and more conscious investors in their own future.

Chapter 7
How behavioral science can lower your energy bill [7]

How many of you have checked your email today? And how about finances? Anybody check that today? Credit card, investment account? How about this week?

Now, how about your household energy use? Anybody check that today? This week? Last week? we aren't paying attention to the energy use that's driving climate change. a woman called Harriet. We met her on our first family vacation. Harriet's paying attention to her energy use, and she is decidedly not an energy geek. This is the story of how Harriet came to pay attention.

This is coal, the most common source of electricity on the planet, and there's enough energy in this coal to light this bulb for more than a year. But unfortunately, between here and here, most of that energy is lost to

---

[7] alex laskey: energy software maker.

things like transmission leakage and heat. In fact, only 10 percent ends up as light. So, this coal will last a little bit more than a month. If you wanted to light this bulb for a year, you'd need this much coal. The bad news here is that, for every unit of energy we use, we waste nine. That means there's good news, because for every unit of energy we save, we save the other nine. So the question is, how can we get the people in this room and across the globe to start paying attention to the energy we're using, and start wasting less of it?

The answer comes from a behavioral science experiment that was run one hot summer, 10 years ago, and only 90 miles from here, in San Marcos, California. Graduate students put signs on every door in a neighborhood, asking people to turn off their air conditioning and turn on their fans. One quarter of the homes received a message that said, did you know you could save 54 dollars a month this summer? Turn off your air conditioning, turn on your fans. Another group got an environmental message. And still a third group got a message about being good citizens, preventing blackouts. Most people guessed that money-saving message would work best of all. In fact, none of these messages worked. They had zero impact on energy consumption. It was as if the grad students hadn't shown up at all.

But there was a fourth message, and this message simply said, "When surveyed, 77 percent of your neighbors said that they turned off their air conditioning and turned on their fans. Please join them. Turn off your air conditioning and turn on your fans." And wouldn't you know it, they did. The people who received this message showed a marked decrease in energy consumption simply by being told what their neighbors were doing.

So, what does this tell us? Well, if something is inconvenient, even if we believe in it, moral suasion, financial incentives, don't do much to move us -- but social pressure, that's powerful stuff. And harnessed correctly, it can be a powerful force for good. In fact, it already is.

Inspired by this insight, my friend Dan Yates and I started a company called Opower. We built software and partnered with utility companies who wanted to help their customers save energy. We deliver personalized home energy reports that show people how their consumption compares to their neighbors in similar-sized homes. Just like those effective door hangers, we have people comparing themselves to their neighbors, and then we give everyone targeted recommendations to help them save. We started with paper, we moved to a mobile application, web, and now even a controllable thermostat, and for the last five years we've been running the largest behavioral science experiment in the world.

And it's working. Ordinary homeowners and renters have saved more than

250 million dollars on their energy bills, and we're just getting started. This year alone, in partnership with more than 80 utilities in six countries, we're going to generate another two-terawatt hour of electricity savings.

Now, the energy geeks in the room know two terawatt hours, but for the rest of us, two terawatt hours is more than enough energy to power every home in St. Louis and Salt Lake City combined for more than a year. Two terawatt hours, it's roughly half what the U.S. solar industry produced last year. And two terawatt hours? In terms of coal, we'd need to burn 34 of these wheelbarrows every minute around the clock every day for an entire year to get two terawatt hours of electricity. And we're not burning anything. We're just motivating people to pay attention and change their behavior.

But we're just one company, and this is just scratching the surface. Twenty percent of the electricity in homes is wasted, and when I say wasted, I don't mean that people have inefficient lightbulbs. They may. I mean we leave the lights on in empty rooms, and we leave the air conditioning on when nobody's home. That's 40 billion dollars a year wasted on electricity that does not contribute to our well-being but does contribute to climate change. That's 40 billion -- with a B -- every year in the U.S. alone. That's half our coal usage right there.

Now thankfully, some of the world's best material scientists are looking to replace coal with sustainable resources like these, and this is both fantastic and essential. But the most overlooked resource to get us to a sustainable energy future, it isn't on this slide. It's in this room. It's you, and it's me. And we can harness this resource with no new material science simply by applying behavioral science. We can do it today, we know it works, and it will save us money right away.

So, what are we waiting for? Well, in most places, utility regulation hasn't changed much since Thomas Edison. Utilities are still rewarded when their customers waste energy. They ought to be rewarded for helping their customers save it.

But this story is much more than about household energy use. Take a look at the Prius. It's efficient not only because Toyota invested in material science but because they invested in behavioral science. The dashboard that shows drivers how much energy they're saving in real time makes former speed demons drive more like cautious grandmothers.

Which brings us back to Harriet. We met her on our first family vacation. She came over to meet my young daughter, and she was tickled to learn that my daughter's name is also Harriet. She asked me what I did for a living, and I told her, I work with utilities to help people save energy. It was then that her eyes lit up.

She looked at me, and she said, "You're exactly the person I need to talk to. You see, two weeks ago, my husband and I got a letter in the mail from our utility. It told us we were using twice as much energy as our neighbors. And for the last two weeks, all we can think about, talk about, and even argue about, is what we should be doing to save energy. We did everything that letter told us to do, and still I know there must be more. Now I'm here with a genuine expert. Tell me. What should I do to save energy?"

There are many experts who can help answer Harriet's question. My goal is to make sure we are all asking it.

Chapter 8
A smart loan for people with no credit history [8]

How much do you need to know about a person before you'd feel comfortable making a loan?

Suppose you wanted to lend 1,000 dollars to the person sitting two rows behind you. What would you need to know about that person before you'd feel comfortable?

My mom came to the US from India in her late thirties. She's a doctor in Brooklyn, and she often lets friends and neighbors come to see her for health services, whether they can pay right away or not. I remember running into her patients with her at the grocery store or on the sidewalk, and sometimes they would come and pay her right on the spot for previous appointments. She would thank them, and ask them about their families and their health. She gave them credit because she trusted them.

---

[8] Shivani siroya: mobile finance entrepreneur.

Most of us are like my mom. We would give credit to someone we know or that we live next to. But most of us are probably not going to lend to a stranger unless we know a little something about them.

Banks, credit card companies and other financial institutions don't know us on a personal level, but they do have a way of trusting us, and that's through our credit scores. Our credit scores have been created through an aggregation and analysis of our public consumer credit data. And because of them, we have pretty much easy access to all of the goods and services that we need, from getting electricity to buying a home, or taking a risk and starting a business.

But ... there are 2.5 billion people around the world that don't have a credit score. That's a third of the world's population. They don't have a score because there are no formal public records on them -- no bank accounts, no credit histories and no social security numbers. And because they don't have a score, they don't have access to the credit or financial products that can improve their lives. They are not trusted.

So, we wanted to find a way to build trust and to open up financial access for these 2.5 billion. So, we created a mobile application that builds credit scores for them using mobile data. There are currently over one billion smartphones in emerging markets. And people are using them the same way that we do. They're texting their friends, they're looking up directions, they're browsing the Internet and they're even making financial transactions.

Over time, this data is getting captured on our phones, and it provides a really rich picture of a person's life. Our customers give us access to this data and we capture it through our mobile application. It helps us understand the creditworthiness of people like Jenipher, a small-business owner in Nairobi, Kenya. Jenipher is 65 years old, and for decades has been running a food stall in the central business district. She has three sons who she put through vocational school, and she's also the leader of her local chama, or savings group.

Jenipher's food stall does well. She makes just enough every day to cover her expenses. But she's not financially secure. Any emergency could force her into debt. And she has no discretionary income to improve her family's way of living, for emergencies, or for investing into growing her business. If Jenipher wants credit, her options are limited. She could get a microloan, but she'd have to form a group that could help vouch for her credibility. And even then, the loan sizes would be way too small to really have an impact on her business, averaging around 150 dollars. Loan sharks are always an option, but with interest rates that are well above 300 percent, they're financially risky. And because Jenipher doesn't have collateral or a credit history, she can't walk into a bank and ask for a business loan.

But one day, Jenipher's son convinced her to download our application and apply for a loan. Jenipher answered a few questions on her phone and she gave us access to a few key data points on her device.

And here's what we saw. So, bad news first. Jenipher had a low savings balance and no previous loan history. These are factors that would have thrown up a red flag to a traditional bank. But there were other points in her history that showed us a much richer picture of her potential. So, for one, we saw that she made regular phone calls to her family in Uganda. Well, it turns out that the data shows a four percent increase in repayment among people who consistently communicate with a few close contacts. We could also see that though she traveled around a lot throughout the day, she actually had pretty regular travel patterns, and she was either at home or at her food stall. And the data shows a six percent increase in repayment among customers who are consistent with where they spend most of their time.

We could also see that she communicated a lot with many different people throughout the day and that she had a strong support network. Our data shows that people who communicate with more than 58 different contacts tend to be more likely to be good borrowers. In Jenipher's case, she communicated with 89 different individuals, which showed a nine percent increase in her repayment.

These are just some of the thousands of different data points that we look at to understand a person's creditworthiness. And after analyzing all of these different data points, we took the first risk and gave Jenipher a loan. This is data that would not be found on a paper trail or in any formal financial record. But it proves trust. By looking beyond income, we can see that people in emerging markets that may seem risky and unpredictable on the surface are actually willing and have the capacity to repay.

Our credit scores have helped us deliver over 200,000 loans in Kenya in just the past year. And our repayment rates are above 90 percent -- which, by the way, is in line with traditional bank repayment rates.

With something as simple as a credit score, we're giving people the power to build their own futures. Our customers have used their loans for family expenses, emergencies, travel and for investing back into growing their businesses. They're now building better economies and communities where more people can succeed.

Over the past two years of using our product, Jenipher has increased her savings by 60 percent. She's also started two additional food stalls and is now making plans for her own restaurant. She's applying for a small-business loan from a commercial bank, because she now has the credit history to prove she deserves it.

I saw Jenipher in Nairobi just last week, and she told me how excited she was to get started. She said, "Only my son believed I could do this. I didn't think this was for me." She's lived her whole life believing that there was a part of the world that was closed off to her.

Our job now is to open the world to Jenipher and the billions like her that deserve to be trusted.

chapter 9

Does money make you mean? [9]

I want you to, for a moment, think about playing a game of Monopoly. Except in this game, that combination of skill, talent and luck that helped earn you success in games, as in life, has been rendered irrelevant, because this game's been rigged, and you've got the upper hand. You've got more money, more opportunities to move around the board, and more access to resources. And as you think about that experience, I want you to ask yourself: How might that experience of being a privileged player in a rigged game change the way you think about yourself and regard that other player?

So, we ran a study on the UC Berkeley campus to look at exactly that question. We brought in more than 100 pairs of strangers into the lab, and with the flip of a coin, randomly

---

)[9] paul piff: social psychologist.

assigned one of the two to be a rich player in a rigged game. They got two times as much money; when they passed Go, they collected twice the salary; and they got to roll both dice instead of one, so they got to move around the board a lot more.

And over the course of 15 minutes, we watched through hidden cameras what happened.

it was quickly apparent to players that something was up. One person clearly has a lot more money than the other person, and yet, as the game unfolded, we saw very notable differences, dramatic differences begin to emerge between the two players. The rich player started to move around the board louder, literally smacking the board with the piece as he went around.

We were more likely to see signs of dominance and nonverbal signs, displays of power and celebration among the rich players.

We had a bowl of pretzels positioned off to the side. It's on the bottom right corner. That allowed us to watch participants' consummatory behavior. So, we're just tracking how many pretzels participants eat.

so, no surprises, people are on to us. They wonder what that bowl of pretzels is doing there in the first place. One even asks, like you just saw, "Is that bowl of pretzels there as a trick?" And yet, despite that, the power of the situation seems to inevitably dominate, and those rich players start to eat more pretzels.

as the game went on, one of the really interesting and dramatic patterns that we observed begin to emerge was that the rich players actually started to become ruder toward the other person -- less and less sensitive to the plight of those poor, poor players, and more and more demonstrative of their material success, more likely to showcase how well they're doing.

And here's what I think was really, really interesting: it's that, at the end of the 15 minutes, we asked the players to talk about their experience during the game. And when the rich players talked about why they had inevitably won in this rigged game of Monopoly They talked about what they'd done to buy those different properties and earn their success in the game.

And they became far less attuned to all those different features of the situation -- including that flip of a coin -- that had randomly gotten them into that privileged position in the first place. And that's a really, really incredible insight into how the mind makes sense of advantage.

Now, this game of Monopoly can be used as a metaphor for understanding society and its hierarchical structure, wherein some people have a lot of wealth and a lot of status, and a lot of people don't; they have a lot less wealth and a lot less status and a lot less access to valued resources. And what my colleagues and I for the last seven years have been doing is studying the effects of these kinds of hierarchies. What we've been finding across dozens of studies and thousands of participants across this country is that as a person's levels of wealth increase, their feelings of compassion and empathy go down, and their feelings of entitlement, of deservingness, and their ideology of self-interest increase. In surveys, we've found that it's actually wealthier individuals who are more likely to moralize greed being good, and that the pursuit of self-interest is favorable and moral. Now, what I want to do today is talk about some of the implications of this ideology self-interest, talk about why we should care about those implications, and end with what might be done.

Some of the first studies that we ran in this area looked at helping behavior, something social psychologists call "pro-social behavior." And we were really interested in who's more likely to offer help to another person: someone who's rich or someone who's poor. In one of the studies, we bring rich and poor members of the community into the lab, and give each of them the equivalent of 10 dollars. We told the participants they could keep these 10 dollars for themselves, or they could share a portion of it, if they wanted to, with a stranger, who's totally anonymous. They'll never meet that stranger; the stranger will never meet them. And we just monitor how much people give. Individuals who made 25,000, sometimes under 15,000 dollars a year, gave 44 percent more of their money to the stranger than did individuals making 150,000, 200,000 dollars a year.

We've had people play games to see who's more or less likely to cheat to increase their chances of winning a prize. In one of the games, we actually rigged a computer so that die rolls over a certain score were impossible --

You couldn't get above 12 in this game, and yet ... the richer you were, the more likely you were to cheat in this game to earn credits toward a $50 cash prize -- sometimes by three to four times as much.

We ran another study where we looked at whether people would be inclined to take candy from a jar of candy that we explicitly identified as being reserved for children. I know it sounds like I'm making a joke. We explicitly told participants: "This candy is for children participating in a developmental lab nearby. They're in studies. This is for them." And we just monitored how much candy participants took. Participants who felt rich took two times as much candy as participants who felt poor.

We've even studied cars. Not just any cars, but whether drivers of different kinds of cars are more or less inclined to break the law. In one of these studies, we looked at whether drivers would stop for a pedestrian that we had posed waiting to cross at a crosswalk. Now in California, as you all know, because I'm sure we all do this, it's the law to stop for a pedestrian who's waiting to cross. So, here's an example of how we did it. That's our confederate off to the left, posing as a pedestrian. He approaches as the red truck successfully stops. In typical California fashion, it's overtaken by the bus who almost runs our pedestrian over.

Now here's an example of a more expensive car, a Prius, driving through, and a BMW doing the same. So, we did this for hundreds of vehicles on several days, just tracking who stops and who doesn't. What we found was as the expensiveness of a car increased the drivers' tendencies to break the law increased as well. None of the cars -- none of the cars -- in our least expensive car category broke the law. Close to 50 percent of the cars in our most expensive vehicle category broke the law. We've run other studies, finding that wealthier individuals are more likely to lie in negotiations, to endorse unethical behavior at work, like stealing cash from the cash register, taking bribes, lying to customers.

Now, I don't mean to suggest that it's only wealthy people who show these patterns of behavior. Not at all -- in fact, I think that we all, in our day-to-day, minute-by-minute lives, struggle with these competing motivations of when or if to put our own interests above the interests of other people. And that's understandable, because the American dream is an idea in which we all have an equal opportunity to succeed and prosper, as long as we apply ourselves and work hard. And a piece of that means that sometimes, you need to put your own interests above the interests and well-being of other people around you. But what we're finding is that the wealthier you are, the more likely you are to pursue a vision of personal success, of achievement and accomplishment, to the detriment of others around you.

Here I've plotted for you the mean household income received by each fifth and top five percent of the population over the last 20 years. In 1993, the differences between the different quintiles of the population, in terms of income, are fairly egregious. It's not difficult to discern that there are differences. But over the last 20 years, that significant difference has become a Grand Canyon of sorts between those at the top and everyone else. In fact, the top 20 percent of our population own close to 90 percent of the total wealth in this country.

We're at unprecedented levels of economic inequality. What that means is that wealth is not only becoming increasingly concentrated in the hands of a select group of individuals, but the American dream is becoming increasingly unattainable for an increasing majority of us. And if it's the case, as we've been finding, that the wealthier you are, the more entitled you feel to that wealth, and the more likely you are to prioritize your own interests above the interests of other people, and be willing to do things to serve that self-interest, well, then, there's no reason to think that those patterns will change. In fact, there's every reason to think that they'll only get worse, and that's what it would look like if things just stayed the same, at the same linear rate, over the next 20 years.

Now inequality -- economic inequality -- is something we should all be concerned about, and not just because of those at the bottom of the social hierarchy, but because individuals and groups with lots of economic inequality do worse ... not just the people at the bottom, everyone. There's a lot of really compelling research coming out from top labs all over the world, showcasing the range of things that are undermined as economic inequality gets worse. Social mobility, things we really care about, physical health, social trust, all go down as inequality goes up. Similarly, negative things in social collectives and societies, things like obesity, and violence, imprisonment, and punishment, are exacerbated as economic inequality increases. Again, these are outcomes not just experienced by a few, but that resound across all strata of society. Even people at the top experience these outcomes.

So, what do we do? This cascade of self-perpetuating, pernicious, negative effects could seem like something that's spun out of control, and there's nothing we can do about it, certainly nothing we as individuals could do. But in fact, we've been finding in our own laboratory research that small psychological interventions, small changes to people's values, small nudges in certain directions, can restore levels of egalitarianism and empathy. For instance, reminding people of the benefits of cooperation or the advantages of community, cause wealthier individuals to be just as egalitarian as poor people.

In one study, we had people watch a brief video, just 46 seconds long, about childhood poverty that served as a reminder of the needs of others in the world around them. And after watching that, we looked at how willing people were to offer up their own time to a stranger presented to them in the lab, who was in distress. After watching this video, an hour later, rich people became just as generous of their own time to help out this other person, a stranger, as someone who's poor, suggesting that these differences are not innate or categorical, but are so malleable to slight changes in people's values, and little nudges of compassion and bumps of empathy.

And beyond the walls of our lab, we're even beginning to see signs of change in society. Bill Gates, one of our nation's wealthiest individuals, in his Harvard commencement speech, talked about the problem of inequality facing society as being the most daunting challenge, and talked about what must be done to combat it, saying, "Humanity's greatest advances are not in its discoveries -- but in how those discoveries are applied to reduce inequity." And there's the Giving Pledge, in which more than 100 of our nation's wealthiest individuals are pledging half of their fortunes to charity. And there's the emergence of dozens of grassroots movements, like "We are the 1 percent," "Resource Generation," or "Wealth for Common Good," in which the most privileged members of the population, members of the one percent and elsewhere, people who are wealthy, are using their own economic resources, adults and youth alike -- that's what's most striking to me -- leveraging their own privilege, their own economic resources, to combat inequality by advocating for social policies, changes in social values and changes in people's behavior that work against their own economic interests, but that may ultimately restore the American dream.

Chapter 10
How to buy happiness [10]

So, I want to talk about money and happiness, which are two things a lot of us spend a lot of our time thinking about, either trying to earn them or trying to increase them. And a lot of us resonate with this phrase, we see it in religions and self-help books: money can't buy happiness. And I want to suggest today that, in fact, that's wrong.

I'm at a business school, so that's what we do. So that's wrong, and in fact, if you think that, you're just not spending it right. So instead of spending it the way you usually spend it, maybe if you spent it differently, that might work a little bit better. Before I tell you the ways you can spend it that will make you happier, let's think about the ways we usually spend it that don't, in fact, make us happier. We had a little natural experiment. So, CNN, a little while ago, wrote this interesting article on what

---

)[10] Dr. Michael Norton: Happy Money: The Science of Happier Spending, amazon, 2014.

happens to people when they win the lottery. It turns out people think when they win the lottery their lives will be amazing. This article's about how their lives get ruined. What happens when people win the lottery is, one, they spend all the money and go into debt; and two, all of their friends and everyone they've ever met find them and bug them for money. It ruins their social relationships, in fact. So, they have more debt and worse friendships than they had before they won the lottery.

What was interesting about the article was, people started commenting on the article, readers of the thing. And instead of talking about how it made them realize that money doesn't lead to happiness, everyone started saying, "You know what I'd do if I won the lottery ...?" and fantasizing about what they'd do. Here's just two of the ones we saw that are interesting to think about. One person wrote, "When I win, I'm going to buy my own little mountain and have a little house on top."

And another person wrote, "I would fill a big bathtub with money and get in the tub while smoking a big fat cigar and sipping a glass of champagne." This is even worse: "... then I'd have a picture taken and dozens of glossies made. Anyone begging for money or trying to extort from me would receive a copy of the picture and nothing else."

And so many of the comments were exactly of this type, where people got money and, in fact, it made them antisocial. So, I told you it ruins people's lives and their friends bug them. Also, money often makes us feel very selfish and we do things only for ourselves. We thought maybe the reason money doesn't make us happy is that we're spending it on the wrong things; in particular, we're always spending it on ourselves. And we wondered what would happen if we made people spend more of their money on others. So instead of being antisocial with your money, what if you were more pro-social with it?

We thought, let's make people do it and see what happens. Let's have some people do what they usually do, spend money on themselves, and let's make some people give money away, and measure their happiness and see if, in fact, they get happier. The first way we did this was, one Vancouver morning, we went out on the campus at University of British Columbia, approached people and said, "Do you want to be in an experiment?" They said, "Yes." We asked them how happy they were, and then gave them an envelope. One of the envelopes had things in it that said, "By 5pm today, spend this money on yourself." We gave some examples of what you could spend it on. Other people got a slip of paper that said, "By 5pm today, spend this money on somebody else." Also, inside the envelope was money.

And we manipulated how much money we gave them; some people got this slip of paper and five dollars; some got this slip of paper and 20 dollars. We let them go about their day and do whatever they wanted. We found out they did spend it in the way we asked them to. We called them up and asked them, "What did you spend it on? How happy do you feel now?" What did they spend it on? These are college undergrads; a lot of what they spent it on for themselves were things like earrings and makeup. One woman said she bought a stuffed animal for her niece. People gave money to homeless people. Huge effect here of Starbucks.

So, if you give undergraduates five dollars, it looks like coffee to them, and they run over to Starbucks and spend it as fast as they can. Some people bought coffee for themselves, the way they usually would, but others bought coffee for somebody else. So the very same purchase, just targeted toward yourself or targeted toward somebody else. What did we find when we called at the end of the day? People who spent money on others got happier; people who spent it on themselves, nothing happened. It didn't make them less happy; it just didn't do much for them.

The other thing we saw is the amount of money doesn't matter much. People thought 20 dollars would be way better than five. In fact, it doesn't matter how much money you spent. What really matters is that you spent it on somebody else rather than on yourself. We see this again and again when we give people money to spend on others instead of on themselves. Of course, these are undergraduates in Canada -- not the world's most representative population. They're also fairly wealthy and affluent and other sorts of things.

We wanted to see if this holds true everywhere in the world or just among wealthy countries. So, we went to Uganda and ran a very similar experiment. Imagine, instead of just people in Canada, we say, "Name the last time you spent money on yourself or others. Describe it. How happy did it make you?" Or in Uganda, "Name the last time you spent money on yourself or others and describe that." Then we asked them how happy they are, again. And what we see is sort of amazing, because there's human universals on what you do with your money, and real cultural differences on what you do as well. So, for example, one guy from Uganda says this: "I called a girl I wished to love." They basically went out on a date, and he says at the end that he didn't "achieve" her up till now.

Here's a guy from Canada. Very similar thing. "I took my girlfriend out for dinner. We went to a movie, we left early, and then went back to her room for ... cake," just cake.

Human universal: you spend money on others, you're being nice. Maybe you have something in mind, maybe not. But then we see extraordinary differences. So, look at these two. This is a woman from Canada. We say, "Name a time you spent money on somebody

136

else." She says, "I bought a present for my mom. I drove to the mall, bought a present, gave it to my mom." Perfectly nice thing to do. It's good to get gifts for people you know. Compare that to this woman from Uganda: "I was walking and met a longtime friend whose son was sick with malaria. They had no money; they went to a clinic and I gave her this money." This isn't $10,000, it's the local currency. So, it's a very small amount of money, in fact. But enormously different motivations here. This is a real medical need, literally a lifesaving donation. Above, it's just kind of, I bought a gift for my mother.

What we see again, though, is that the specific way you spend on other people isn't nearly as important as the fact that you spend on other people in order to make yourself happy, which is really quite important. So you don't have to do amazing things with your money to make yourself happy. You can do small, trivial things and still get the benefits from doing this. These are only two countries. We wanted to look at every country in the world if we could, to see what the relationship is between money and happiness.

We got data from the Gallup Organization, which you know from all the political polls happening lately. They asked people, "Did you donate money to charity recently?" and, "How happy are you with life in general?" We can see what the relationship is between those two things. Are they positively correlated, giving money makes you happy? Or are they negatively correlated? On this map, green will mean they're positively correlated, red means they're negatively correlated. And you can see, the world is crazily green. So, in almost every country in the world where we have this data, people who give money to charity are happier people than people who don't give money to charity. I know you're looking at the red country in the middle. I would be a jerk and not tell you what it is, but it's Central African Republic. You can make up stories. Maybe it's different there for some reason. Just below that to the right is Rwanda, though, which is amazingly green.

So almost everywhere we look, we see that giving money away makes you happier than keeping it for yourself. What about work, which is where we spend the rest of our time, when we're not with the people we know. We decided to infiltrate some companies and do a very similar thing. These are sales teams in Belgium. They work in teams, go out and sell to doctors and try to get them to buy drugs.

We can look and see how well they sell things as a function of being a member of a team. We give people on some teams some money "Spend it however you want on yourself," just like we did with the undergrads in Canada.

To other teams we say, "Here's 15 euro. Spend it on one of your teammates. Buy them something as a gift and give it to them. Then we can see, we've got teams that spend on themselves and these pro-social teams who we give money to make the team better. The reason I have a ridiculous pinata there is one team pooled their money and bought a pinata, they smashed the pinata, the candy fell out and things like that.

A silly, trivial thing to do, but think of the difference on a team that didn't do that at all, that got 15 euro, put it in their pocket, maybe bought themselves a coffee, or teams that had this pro-social experience where they bonded together to buy something and do a group activity. What we see is that the teams that are pro-social sell more stuff than the teams that only got money for themselves.

One way to think of it is: for every 15 euro you give people for themselves, they put it in their pocket and don't do anything different than before. You don't get money from that; you lose money, since it doesn't motivate them to perform better.

But when you give them 15 euro to spend on their teammates, they do so much better on their teams that you actually get a huge win on investing this kind of money.

You're probably thinking to yourselves; this is all fine, but there's a context that's incredibly important for public policy, and I can't imagine it would work there. And if he doesn't show me that it works here, I don't believe anything he said. I know what you're all thinking about are dodgeball teams.

This was a huge criticism that we got, that if you can't show it with dodgeball teams, this is all stupid. So, we went and found these dodgeball teams and infiltrated them, and did the exact same thing as before. So, we give people on some team's money to spend on themselves.

Other teams, we give them money to spend on their dodgeball teammates. The teams that spend money on themselves have the same winning percentages as before. The teams we give the money to spend on each other become different teams; they dominate the league by the time they're done.

Across all of these different contexts -- your personal life, you work life, even things like intramural sports -- we see spending on other people has a bigger return for you than spending on yourself. So, if you think money can't buy happiness, you're not spending it right. The implication isn't you should buy this product instead of that product, and that's the way to make yourself happier. It's that you should stop thinking about which product to buy for yourself, and try giving some of it to other people instead.

And we luckily have an opportunity for you. DonorsChoose.org is a nonprofit for mainly public-school teachers in low-income schools. They post projects like, "I want to teach Huckleberry Finn and we don't have the books," or, "I want a microscope to teach my students science and we don't have a microscope.

You and I can go on and buy it for them. The teacher and the kids write you thank-you notes, sometimes they send pictures of them using the microscope. It's an extraordinary thing.

Go to the website and start yourself on the process of thinking less about "How can I spend money on myself?" and more about "If I've got five dollars or 15 dollars, what can I do to benefit other people?" Ultimately, when you do that, you'll find you benefit yourself much more.

Chapter 11
Should you donate differently? [11]

I suspect that every aid worker in Africa comes to a time in her career when she wants to take all the money for her project — maybe it's a school or a training program — pack it in a suitcase, get on a plane flying over the poorest villages in the country, and start throwing that money out the window. Because to a veteran aid worker, the idea of putting cold, hard cash into the hands of the poorest people on Earth doesn't sound crazy, it sounds really satisfying.

I had that moment right about the 10-year mark, and luckily, that's also when I learned that this idea actually exists, and it might be just what the aid system needs. Economists call it an unconditional cash transfer, and it's exactly that: Its cash given with no strings attached. Governments in developing countries have been doing this for decades, and

---

)[11] joy sun: veteran aid worker.

it's only now, with more evidence and new technology that it's possible to make this a model for delivering aid. It's a pretty simple idea, right?

Well, why did I spend a decade doing other stuff for the poor? Honestly, I believed that I could do more good with money for the poor than the poor could do for themselves. I held two assumptions: One, that poor people are poor in part because they're uneducated and don't make good choices; two is that we then need people like me to figure out what they need and get it to them. It turns out, the evidence says otherwise. In recent years, researchers have been studying what happens when we give poor people cash. Dozens of studies show across the board that people use cash transfers to improve their own lives. Pregnant women in Uruguay buy better food and give birth to healthier babies. Sri Lankan men invest in their businesses. Researchers who studied our work in Kenya found that people invested in a range of assets, from livestock to equipment to home improvements, and they saw increases in income from business and farming one year after the cash was sent. None of these studies found that people spend more on drinking or smoking or that people work less. In fact, they work more.

Now, these are all material needs. In Vietnam, elderly recipients used their cash transfers to pay for coffins. As someone who wonders if Maslow got it wrong, I find this choice to prioritize spiritual needs deeply humbling. I don't know if I would have chosen to give food or equipment or coffins, which begs the question: How good are we at allocating resources on behalf of the poor? Are we worth the cost? Again, we can look at empirical evidence on what happens when we give people stuff of our choosing. One very telling study looked at a program in India that gives livestock to the so-called ultra-poor, and they found that 30 percent of recipients had turned around and sold the livestock they had been given for cash. The real irony is, for every 100 dollars' worth of assets this program gave someone, they spent another 99 dollars to do it. What if, instead, we use technology to put cash, whether from aid agencies or from any one of us directly into a poor person's hands. Today, three in four Kenyans use mobile money, which is basically a bank account that can run on any cell phone. A sender can pay a 1.6 percent fee and with the click of a button send money directly to a recipient's account with no intermediaries. Like the technologies that are disrupting industries in our own lives, payments technology in poor countries could disrupt aid. It's spreading so quickly that it's possible to imagine reaching billions of the world's poor this way.

That's what we've started to do at Give Directly. We're the first organization dedicated to providing cash transfers to the poor. We've sent cash to 35,000 people across rural Kenya and Uganda in one-time payments of 1,000 dollars per family. So far, we've looked for the poorest people in the poorest villages, and in this part of the world, they're the ones living in homes made of mud and thatch, not cement and iron. So, let's say that's your family. We show up at your door with an Android phone. We'll get your name, take your photo and a photo of your hut and grab the GPS coordinates. That night, we send all the data to the cloud, and each piece gets checked by an independent team using, for one example, satellite images. Then, we'll come back, we'll sell you a basic cell phone if you don't have one already, and a few weeks later, we send money to it. Something that five years ago would have seemed impossible we can now do efficiently and free of corruption.

The more cash we give to the poor, and the more evidence we have that it works, the more we have to reconsider everything else we give. Today, the logic behind aid is too often, well, we do at least some good. When we're complacent with that as our bar, when we tell ourselves that giving aid is better than no aid at all, we tend to invest inefficiently, in our own ideas that strike us as innovative, on writing reports, on plane tickets and SUVs. What if the logic was, will we do better than cash given directly? Organizations would have to prove that they're doing more good for the poor than the poor can do for themselves. Of course, giving cash won't create public goods like eradicating disease or building strong institutions, but it could set a higher bar for how we help individual families improve their lives.

I believe in aid. I believe most aid is better than just throwing money out of a plane. I am also absolutely certain that a lot of aid today isn't better than giving directly to the poor. I hope that one day, it will be.

References

1. Shivani siroya: mobile finance entrepreneur.
2. Daniel Kahneman: Thinking, Fast and Slow. Amazon, 2013.
3. Daniel goldstiein: behavioral economist.
4. shlomo benartzi: economist.
5. paul piff: social psychologist.
6. Michael Norton: Happy Money: The Science of Happier Spending, amazon, 2014.
7. joy sun: veteran aid worker.
8. alex laskey: energy software maker.
9. Elizabeth white: 55, Underemployed, and Faking Normal: Your Guide to a Better Life. Amazon, 2019
10.   tammy lally: money coach.
11.   keith chen: behavioral economist.